PIANO / VOCAL / GUITAR

SHAWN MENDES ILLUMINATE

ISBN 978-1-4950-7878-1

HAL•LEONARD®

7777 W. BLUEMOUND RD. P.O. BOX 13819 MILWAUKEE, WI 53213

Visit Hal Leonard Online at
www.halleonard.com

RUIN

Words and Music by SHAWN MENDES, IDO ZMISHLANY,
SCOTT HARRIS, GEOFFREY WARBURTON
and ZUBIN THAKKAR

MERCY

Words and Music by SHAWN MENDES,
TEDDY GEIGER, DANNY PARKER
and ILSEY JUBER

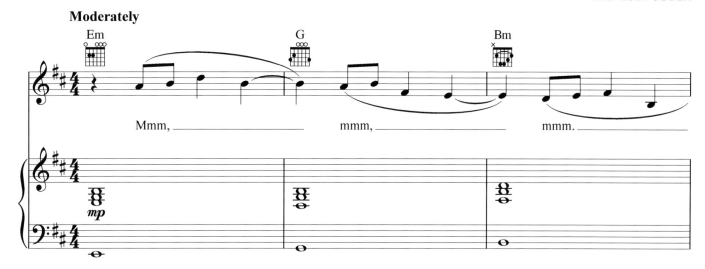

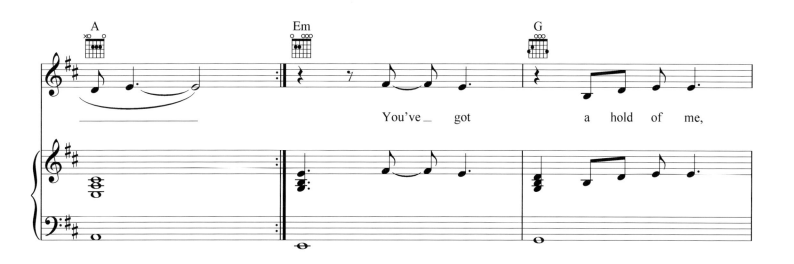

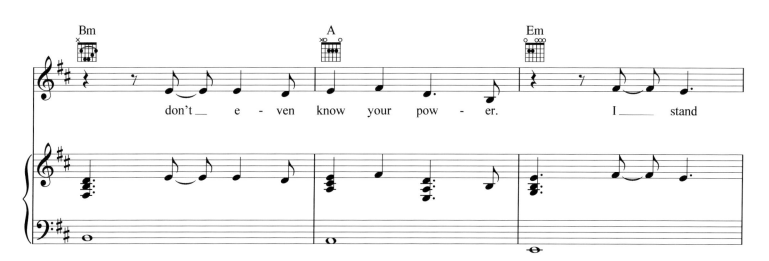

TREAT YOU BETTER

Words and Music by SHAWN MENDES,
SCOTT HARRIS and TEDDY GEIGER

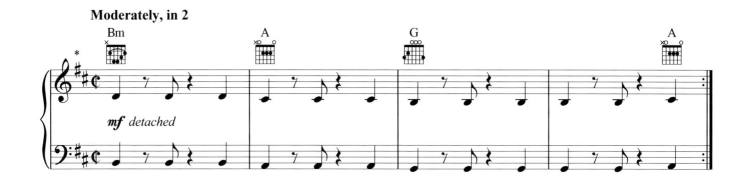

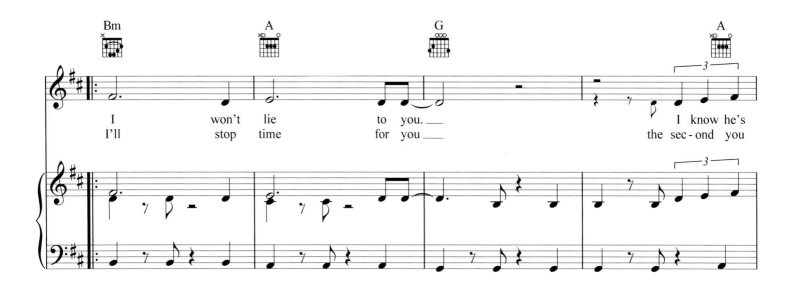

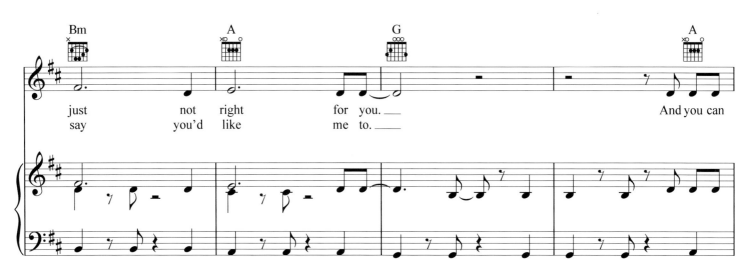

* Recorded a half step lower.

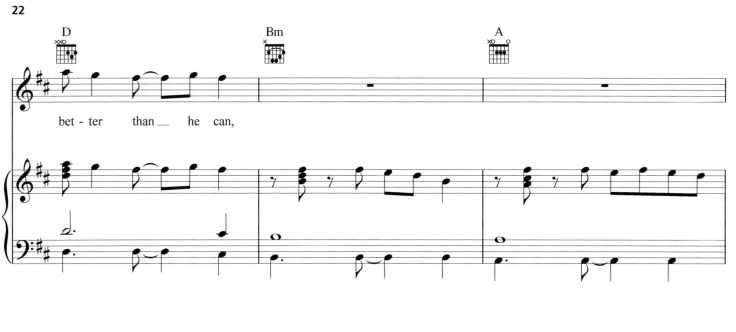

better than — he can,

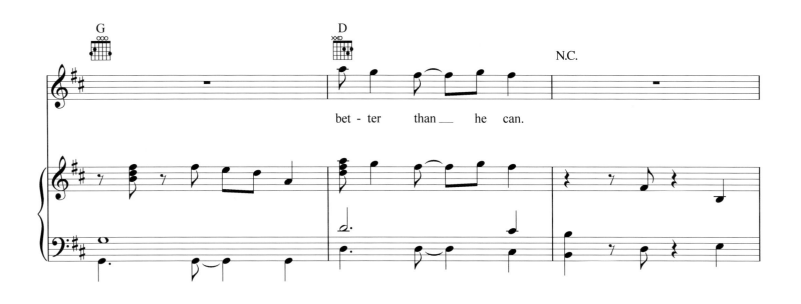

better than — he can.

THREE EMPTY WORDS

Words and Music by SHAWN MENDES,
IDO ZMISHLANY, SCOTT HARRIS
and GEOFFREY WARBURTON

DON'T BE A FOOL

Words and Music by SHAWN MENDES,
SCOTT HARRIS and GEOFFREY WARBURTON

Moderate Waltz

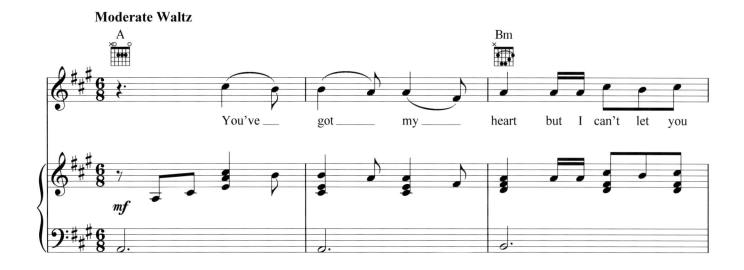

You've ___ got ___ my ___ heart but I can't let you

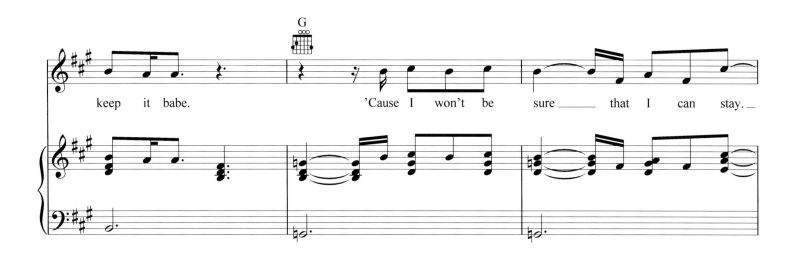

keep it babe. 'Cause I won't be sure ___ that I can stay. ___

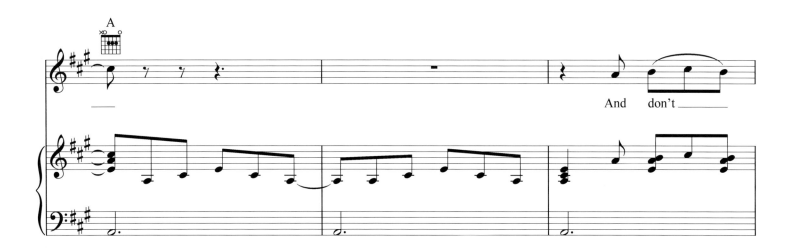

And don't ___

LIKE THIS

Words and Music by SHAWN MENDES,
LALEH POURKARIM and GUSTAF THÖRN

NO PROMISES

Words and Music by SHAWN MENDES,
SCOTT HARRIS, TEDDY GEIGER
and GEOFFREY WARBURTON

LIGHTS ON

Words and Music by SHAWN MENDES,
SCOTT HARRIS and GEOFFREY WARBURTON

Laid-back groove

Ha, _

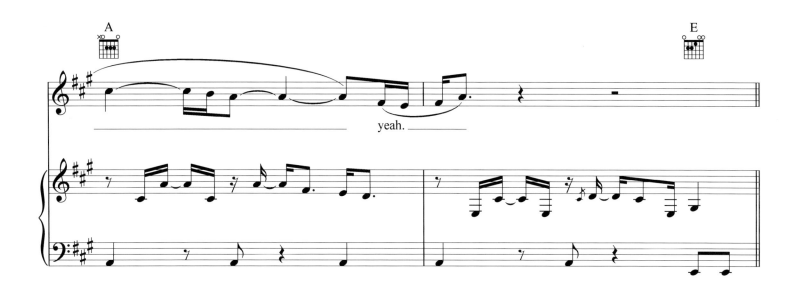

yeah. _____

Damn, you look so good with your clothes on. _
I like the vibe in this ho-tel room. _

D.S. al Coda

I ___ want to see ___ ev-'ry inch of you, ___ I get lost ___ in the way you move. ___ I want to love you with the

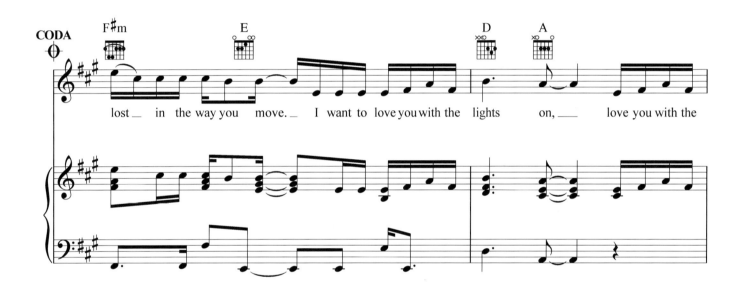

CODA

lost ___ in the way you move. ___ I want to love you with the lights on, ___ love you with the

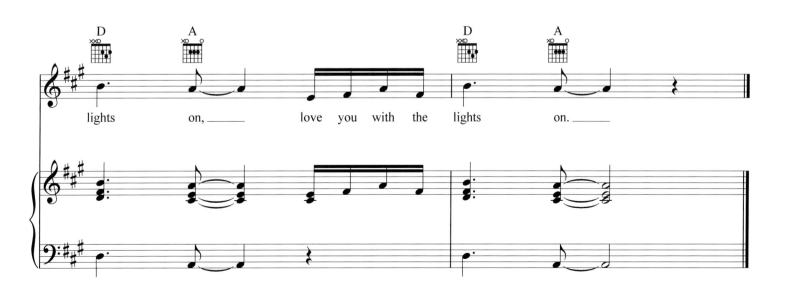

lights on, ___ love you with the lights on. ___

HONEST

Words and Music by SHAWN MENDES
and SCOTT HARRIS

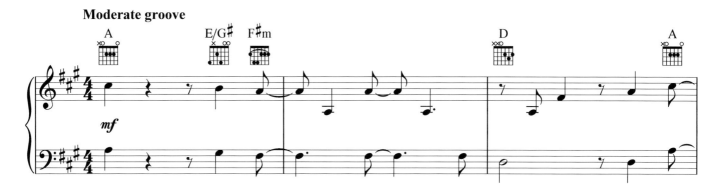

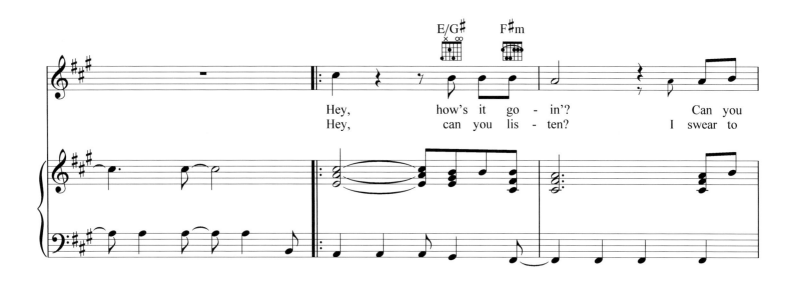

Hey,   how's it go - in'?   Can you
Hey,   can you lis - ten?   I swear to

meet me down on Ad - el - aide street? _____   Can you talk _____   for a mo -
God to you there's no - bod - y else. _____   You're gon - na say _____   that I'm ly -

56

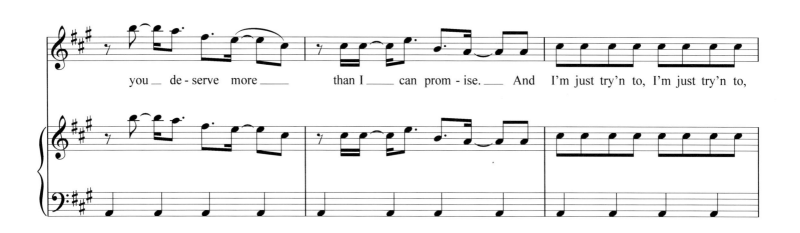

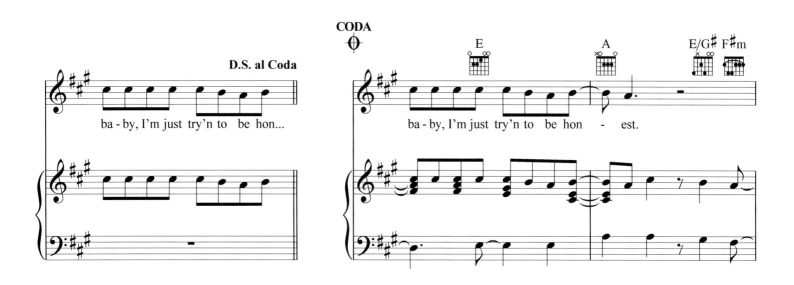

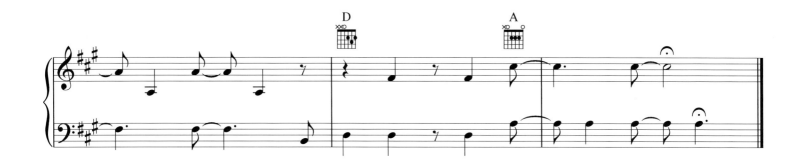

HOLD ON

Words and Music by SHAWN MENDES,
SCOTT HARRIS and GEOFFREY WARBURTON

Stop, take it in ___ and I breathe for a min-ute. I think ___ too much when I'm ___ a-lone. ___ I nev-er win ___ when I keep all my thoughts ___ in-side.

* *Recorded a half step lower.*

PATIENCE

Words and Music by SHAWN MENDES,
SCOTT HARRIS and TEDDY GEIGER

will and then you say you won't. Can you make your mind up? Please, I'm los-ing my pa-tience.

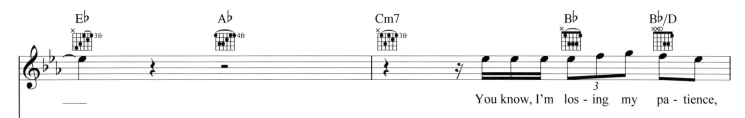

You know, I'm los-ing my pa-tience,

yeah.   And you've got to

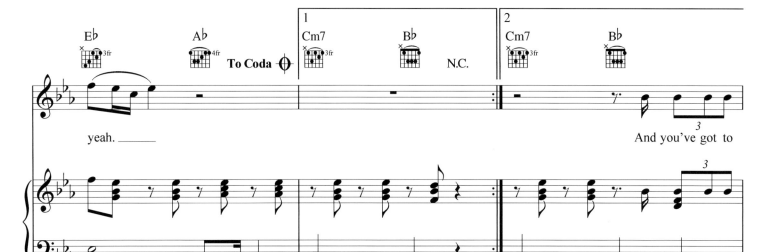

stop   if you know   so I can start   let-ting

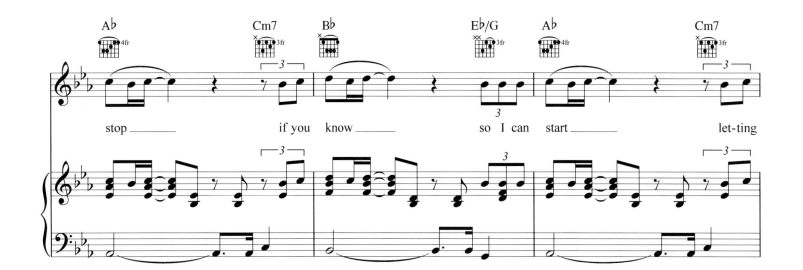

BAD REPUTATION

Words and Music by SHAWN MENDES,
SCOTT HARRIS and GEOFFREY WARBURTON

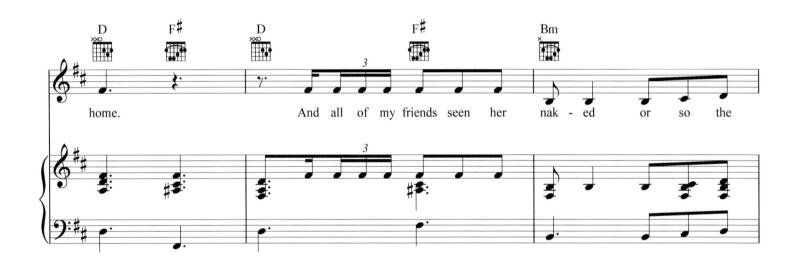

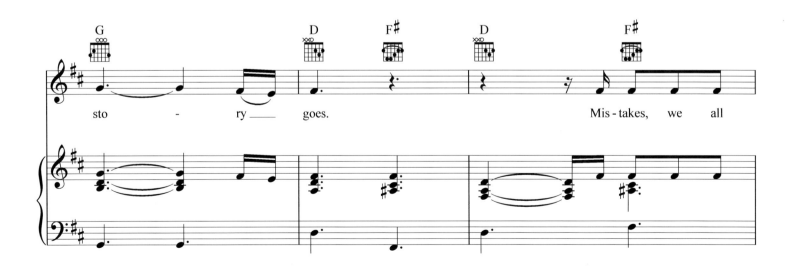

To Coda

UNDERSTAND

Words and Music by SHAWN MENDES,
SCOTT HARRIS, GEOFFREY WARBURTON
and TEDDY GEIGER

Moderate Gospel feel

Am I ask-ing all these ques-tions for noth - ing?
I'm call-ing all my friends af - ter mid - night

I'm won-der-ing if an-y-one's there, ___ yeah.
to re-mind them that I'll al-ways be there _____ for them. _

And I real-ly need to make a con-fes-sion,
It gets lone-ly when there's no one to talk to,

Spoken: (See additional lyrics)

Play 4 times

And ev-'ry time I ask my - self, "Am I turn-ing in - to some - one else?"

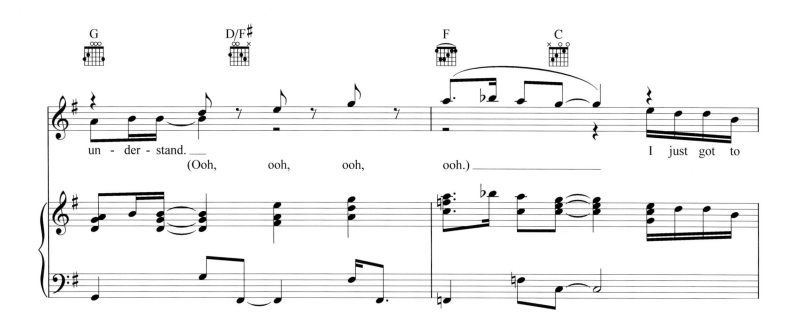

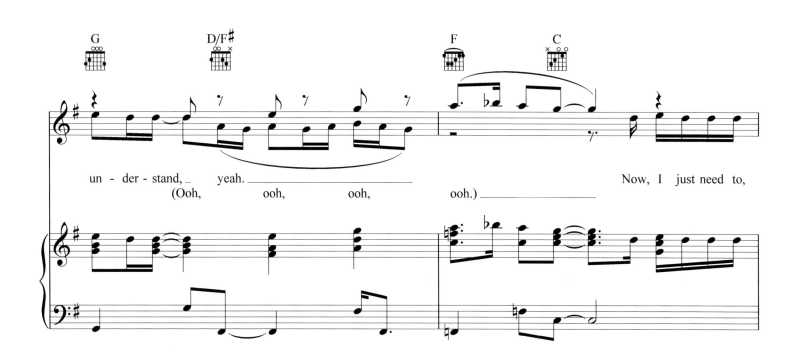

I need to un-der-stand. _ I real-ly want to
(Ooh, ooh, ooh, ooh.) _____

un - der - stand _ oh, _____ who I am. _
(Ooh, ooh, ooh, ooh.) _____

Additional Lyrics

When you wake up your whole world's flipped
It's just different, and you gotta, you know you gotta
You gotta go with it
And that's just simply growing up
And not see it in a negative way
If they see it as it has been given you
I mean, as much as times can be crazy
You're gonna feel like that's where you're supposed to be
You're not going to feel out of place anymore
You're going to feel like that's where you meant to be
You don't have to pretend that it's easy all the time
You just let it go, and, and grow with it
And you can't hold on to the old you, or the old this, or the old that
Because you know you change, and it's not changing in a bad way
It's just changing because that's what happens in life
You grow up, everyone moves on
You're just learning
You stay true to yourself

Changing isn't a bad thing
It never was
But at the end of the day, you know
You're the same person
And, and where your heart is
That doesn't change

ROSES

Words and Music by SHAWN MENDES,
TOM HULL and TOBIAS JESSO

Will you let it die or let it grow? ___ I'm not try'n' to start a fire

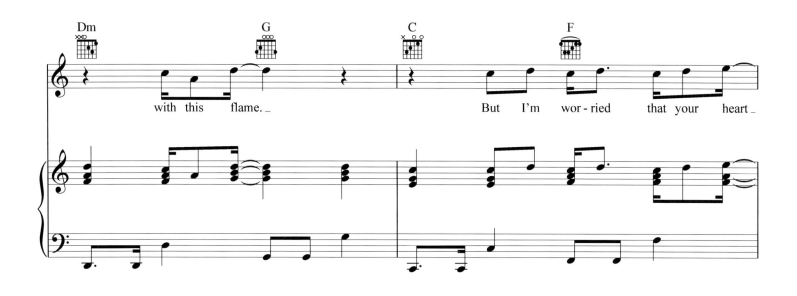

with this flame. _ But I'm wor-ried that your heart _

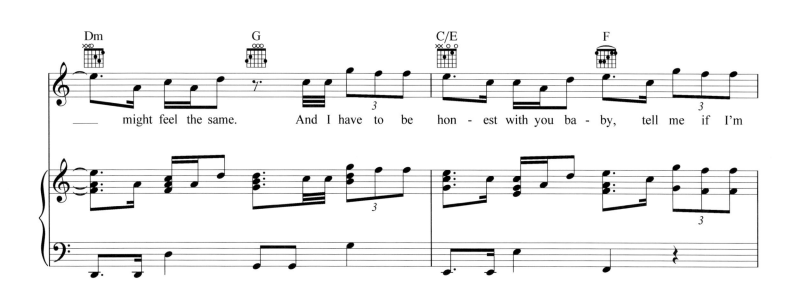

___ might feel the same. And I have to be hon-est with you ba-by, tell me if I'm

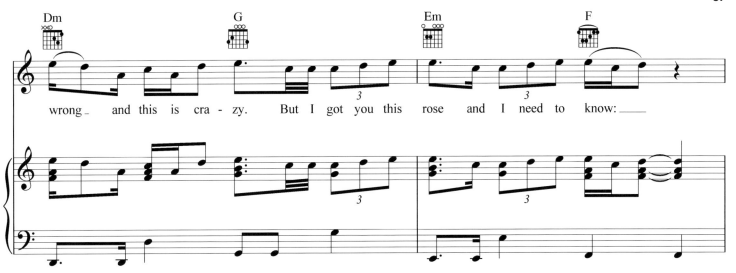

wrong _ and this is cra - zy. But I got you this rose and I need to know: ____

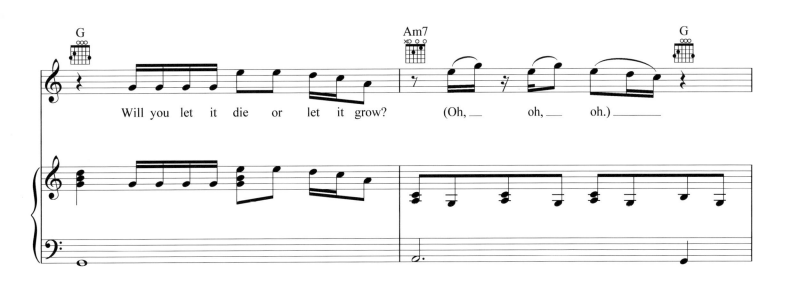

Will you let it die or let it grow? (Oh, __ oh, __ oh.) ____

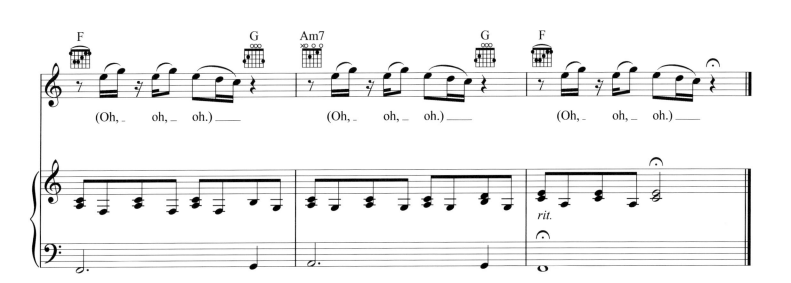

(Oh, _ oh, _ oh.) ____ (Oh, _ oh, _ oh.) (Oh, _ oh, _ oh.) ____